Biomes
of North
America

A Journey into the Ocean

by Rebecca L. Johnson

with illustrations by Phyllis V. Saroff

CAROLRHODA BOOKS, INC./MINNEAPOLIS

Carolrhoda Books, Inc.
A division of Lerner Publishing Group
241 First Avenue North
Minneapolis, Minnesota 55401 U.S.A.

Website address: www.lernerbooks.com

Library of Congress Cataloging-in-Publication Data

Johnson, Rebecca L.
    A journey into the ocean / by Rebecca L. Johnson ; with
illustrations by Phyllis V. Saroff.
       p.   cm. — (Biomes of North America)
    Summary: Takes readers on a journey into the ocean, showing
examples of how the animals and plants of the ocean are connected
and dependent on each other and the ocean's saltwater
environment.
    ISBN: 1-57505-591-0 (lib. bdg. : alk. paper)
    1. Marine ecology—Juvenile literature. 2. Ocean—Juvenile
literature. [1. Marine ecology. 2. Ocean. 3. Ecology.] I. Saroff,
Phyllis V., ill. II. Title. III. Series.
QH541.5.S3J64 2004
577.7—dc22   2003015089

Manufactured in the United States of America
1 2 3 4 5 6 - JR - 09 08 07 06 05 04

Words
to Know

ALGAE *(AL-jee)*—plant-like living things that use sunlight to make their own food

BACTERIA *(bak-TEE-ree-uh)* microscopic, one-celled living things found almost everywhere

COPEPOD *(koh-puh-PAHD)*—a very small hard-bodied ocean animal with many pairs of tiny legs

CURRENT—steady movement of water in a particular direction

FOOD WEB—connections among living things, showing what eats what in an ecosystem

HYDROTHERMAL VENT *(hy-druh-THUR-muhl)*—a crack in the ocean floor that hot, mineral-rich water gushes out of

PLANKTON *(PLANK-tuhn)*—a collection of tiny organisms that drift through the ocean. Plankton are eaten by many ocean animals.

POLYP *(PAH-luhp)*—a single coral animal

PREY *(PRAY)*—an animal that is hunted and eaten by other animals

PREDATOR *(PREH-duh-tur)*—an animal that hunts and eats other animals

REEF—a hard structure made up of the remains of dead corals. A layer of living corals grows on the surface of the reef.

SHORE—land at the edge of the ocean

TIDE—the regular movement of the whole ocean slowly toward the land or away from it

WATER BIOME *(BYE-ohm)*—a water-based region that is home to a special group of living things

breaking on the shore

It's just before dawn, and the dark sky is growing light. *Whoosh!* A wave surges up the beach, then rolls back with a soft hissing sound. A few feet from the water, a tiny flipper pokes out of the sand. Then comes a head and another flipper. With a final push, the baby sea turtle squirms free. One by one, more little turtles wriggle up from beneath the sand. They've just hatched from the eggs their mother laid many weeks ago. They scurry down the beach, toward the waves and the vast ocean beyond.

The ocean stretches to the horizon, where water and sky seem to meet. The ocean is never still. Waves move endlessly over its surface. Sometimes the waves are small. Sometimes they are huge.

Waves form when wind blows across the ocean's surface, making small ripples (below). *As the wind blows harder, the ripples grow into waves* (right).

The ocean seems to change color too. On sunny days, the water is a bright, sparkling blue. On cloudy days, it turns to steely gray. Like a mirror, the ocean reflects the oranges and reds of a sunrise and the warm yellow light of the full moon.

The ocean reflects the colors of the rising sun.

The ocean is enormous. It covers nearly 75 percent of the earth's surface. And it contains 97 percent of the world's water. But you wouldn't want to drink a lot of ocean water. It's very salty.

On land, you can find many smaller bodies of water. There are freshwater lakes and rivers. There are soggy areas of ground called wetlands. And there are estuaries, where salty ocean water and fresh river water meet.

From space, it is easy to see that the ocean covers much of the earth's surface.

Lakes, rivers, wetlands, estuaries, and the ocean make up the earth's water biomes. A water biome is a water-based region that is home to a unique group of living things. These living things are all adapted, or specially suited, to living in that region.

In and around a river (left), plants and animals are adapted to life in fast-moving freshwater. Those that live beside or in a lake (below) are adapted to a still, freshwater home. Estuary dwellers (bottom) live where saltwater and freshwater mix.

Each biome's living things, from tiny microscopic creatures to large plants and animals, form a community. Each member of that community depends on the other members. All these living things, in turn, depend on the water—fresh or salty, moving or still—that forms their watery home. They swim through it, find food in it, and are carried from place to place by it. Without the water, they could not survive.

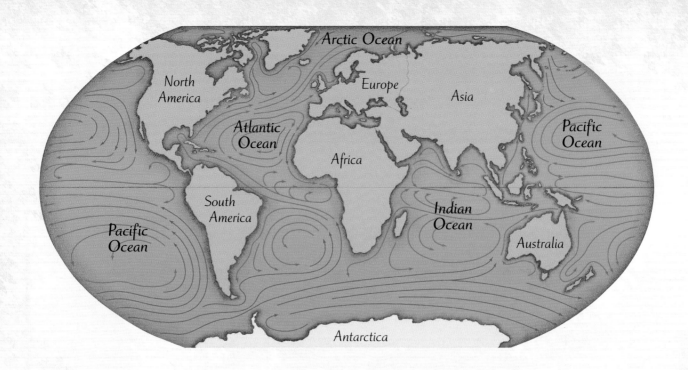

North America

Arctic Ocean

Europe

Asia

Atlantic Ocean

Pacific Ocean

Africa

South America

Pacific Ocean

Indian Ocean

Australia

Antarctica

Although oceans are labeled as separate bodies of water (above), the ocean is really one single body of water that circles the planet. Currents move warm water (green) and cool water (purple) to other parts of the ocean. Near the South Pole, penguins play on floating icebergs (below).

The ocean is by far the largest water biome. On a map of the world, different parts of the ocean have different names. But these parts are all connected. The ocean is really one single body of water that encircles the planet.

That doesn't mean that the ocean is the same everywhere. In some places, the water is shallow. In others, it is several miles deep. Near the equator, the ocean is warm. But near the poles, it is very cold. Huge chunks of ice called icebergs float in chilly polar waters.

From shore, the ocean might not seem very interesting—just waves rolling on and on. But beneath the surface, the ocean is full of life. The newly hatched sea turtles are heading into this salty, wet world for the first time. Let's follow one of them on a journey into the ocean.

Warm ocean waters surround islands near the equator.

Crabs catch and hold their prey with big, pointed front claws.

The sea turtle hurries toward the ocean, trying to avoid crabs, birds, and other predators on the shore.

Using her tiny flippers, the baby sea turtle scoots down the beach. She leaves a dimpled track in the smooth sand.

The turtle hurries past a small, round hole in the sand. The hole is the entrance to a crab's underground home. Crabs eat baby turtles. But this turtle is lucky. The crab that lives here is out hunting for food farther up the beach.

As the sea turtle nears the water, a big wave surges toward her. For a moment, she disappears in a swirl of foam. Then the wave retreats. The turtle rests for a moment on the damp sand.

Waves break against the shore every few seconds. But ocean water moves in other ways too. Twice a day, the edge of the water slowly comes up higher on the shore. Then it gradually moves back out toward the horizon. The "coming in" and "going out" of the ocean is called a tide. When the water comes in, it's high tide. When the water goes out, it's low tide.

A beach at high tide (above) and low tide (below). Tides are caused mostly by the pull of the moon as it orbits the earth.

13

Rounded air bladders help seaweed float near the ocean's surface. There they can get enough sunlight to grow.

Some seaweeds grow as long, leathery straps. Others have lacy branches.

It's high tide on the turtle's beach. The waves reach far up onto the shore. As another big wave rolls in, the baby turtle hurries toward it. The swirling saltwater surrounds her. It lifts her up off the sand. She starts to swim, paddling hard with her flippers. Suddenly free of the land, she heads into the ocean.

The water close to shore is shallow. The turtle glides over a patch of seaweed. The seaweed sways back and forth in the surging water. These plants use sunlight to make their own food, just like plants on land. They, in turn, are food for many ocean animals that live near the shore.

When the tide goes out, the seaweed is exposed to the air for several hours. But it can survive until the water returns. The seaweed has a coating of slime. The slime holds water and keeps the plants from drying out at low tide.

Hermit crabs nibble on seaweed for food. They live in the empty shells of other ocean animals.

Barnacles sweep the water with feathery legs to snare tiny bits of food.

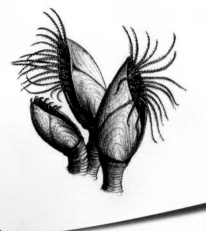

Mussels and barnacles (above) cling so tightly to rocks that waves cannot wash them off. A sea star (right) slithers past spiny sea urchins. Curved into a crevice, a chiton (right inset) hangs on.

Beyond the seaweed, the bottom is rocky. Clinging to the rocks are all sorts of small animals. Every surging wave threatens to tug them off. But the animals have remarkable ways of hanging on.

Barnacles glue themselves to the rocks. So do chunky anemones topped with waving tentacles. Mussels attach to the rocks with tough, sticky threads. Hard-shelled limpets and snails have a big, muscular foot that grips the rocks very tightly—so tightly that they are almost impossible to pry off.

16

The baby turtle swims past a big chiton. Like limpets and snails, the chiton clings to the rocks with a strong foot. Nearby, a five-armed sea star hugs a rocky ledge.

Sea stars use tiny tube feet on the undersides of their arms to cling to rocks.

At low tide, an anemone pulls in its tentacles (right) and waits for the water to return.

A limpet perches on a ledge at low tide.

When the tide goes out and the rocks are exposed, barnacles and mussels retreat into tightly closed shells. Anemones pull in their tentacles. Limpets and chitons clamp down to create an airtight seal.

18

Snails and sea stars creep into tiny pools of water left behind among the rocks. But there is no escape from these tide pools. The ocean animals are easy targets for hungry crabs and sharp-billed shorebirds looking for a meal.

A snail caught out of the water at low tide can close off the opening to its shell with a thin plate that is hard like a fingernail.

Sea stars trapped in a tide pool are easy prey for a lucky shorebird.

19

As the sea turtle swims farther from shore, the water gets deeper. It's more than one hundred feet down to the bottom. Yet there is life all around. The water is teeming with billions of tiny living things. Some are plantlike cells called algae. Others are tiny animals. Together they make up what's known as plankton.

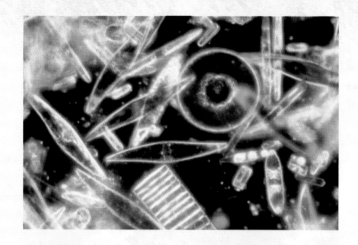

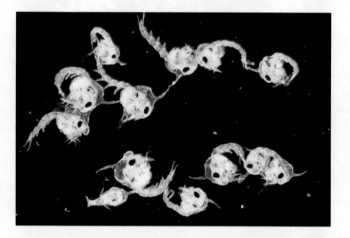

Like seaweeds, tiny algae (top) *in plankton use sunlight to make their own food. Some animal plankton* (middle and bottom) *have bulging eyes and many legs.*

The baby sea turtle eats plankton as she swims along. So do many of the small fish that pass by.

Small fish—and baby turtles—can become food for ocean predators like squid and big fish. Big fish, in turn, are eaten by even bigger fish. Together, all of these living things form a complex food web. Each member of the food web depends on other members for its survival.

Mackerel try to flee a hungry shark. Some sharks feed on mackerel, and mackerel feed on smaller fish that eat plankton.

Corals, like this elkhorn coral, grow only in warm ocean waters.

To hide from predators, the little turtle swims into a clump of floating seaweed. She rests on the surface for a while, drifting farther and farther from land.

An ocean current carries the turtle past a coral reef. The reef is created by billions of tiny animals called coral polyps. As a polyp grows, it builds a stony cup around its soft body. Groups of polyps form rocklike corals. Corals come in all sorts of shapes, sizes, and colors.

Most corals are formed by many coral polyps that live together in groups. During the day, polyps retract into their stony cups (top). At night, they extend their tiny tentacles to feed on plankton (middle).

23

The reef is overflowing with life. Sponges sprout from between corals. Nudibranchs—cousins of snails—crawl slowly along. Anemones huddle in clusters like bright bouquets of flowers.

Sponges are animals that pump water through their bodies and filter out plankton for food.

A nudibranch crawls over a group of sea anemones. A blue sponge (inset) looks like a flower vase.

Spindle-legged lobsters hide under ledges. Octopuses and moray eels lurk in holes, waiting until dark to come out to hunt.

Two spiny lobsters (above) peer out from their home on the reef. Long-legged cleaner shrimp share a hiding place with a moray eel (left).

Hundreds of kinds of fish live around the coral reef too. Many have polka dots, stripes, or swirls in neon-bright colors. Some swim alone. Others move through the reef in groups called schools.

Clownfish live among the stinging tentacles of large anemones (top). *A queen angelfish* (above) *scans the corals for food. Motionless, a stonefish* (left) *blends into the reef.*

Reef fish flash and shimmer in the sunlit waters as they swim around, looking for food. With sharp front teeth, rainbow-colored parrot fish munch on coral. Clownfish dart in and out from the sheltering tentacles of anemones. An elegant angelfish nibbles a bit of seaweed. It glides past a stonefish that looks just like a lump of coral.

When danger threatens, a porcupine fish gulps water and swells up like a giant pincushion.

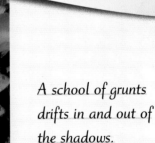

A school of grunts drifts in and out of the shadows.

27

Fish use gills, hidden beneath flaps of scaly skin, to "breathe" underwater.

The open ocean lies beyond the reef. Here hurricanes are born, and huge waves can roll on and on.

Safely hidden in her seaweed raft, the sea turtle rides the current past the reef. Beneath her, the ocean floor angles down sharply, like a cliff. The water is suddenly very deep. The bottom is a mile or more down. This is the vast open ocean, far from land in every direction.

A school of large, silver-sided fish flashes by. Sleek and streamlined, the fish are moving very fast. Are they chasing down a meal? Or are they trying to avoid becoming one?

Bluefin tuna streak through the water at high speed.

A great white shark shows off a mouthful of terrifying teeth.

From out of the blue, a torpedo-shaped shark appears. Some kinds of sharks are the largest fish in the ocean. Most are powerful hunters, armed with rows of razor-sharp teeth. They will eat almost anything they can catch.

The shark passes so close that the turtle can see its jet-black eyes. But the shark doesn't see the turtle, and so it swims on.

The turtle senses movement far down in the water. Something is coming up from below. It's a jellyfish—a shimmering blob trailing long tentacles.

The jellyfish looks harmless, but its tentacles are covered with deadly stinging cells. And baby sea turtles are among its prey. The turtle paddles hard to get away. When she is full grown, however, the tables will be turned—jellyfish will be one of her favorite foods.

When jellyfish pull together their rounded tops, they move up in the water. When they relax, they drift slowly downward.

Whales are not fish, but air-breathing mammals that must come to the surface to breathe.

From somewhere in the distance come strange sounds. Some are long wails. Others are low rumbles. Humpback whales are singing to each other.

One by one, the whales rise to the water's surface. They breathe out with a loud hiss of spray from the blowholes on top of their heads. Then they fill their lungs with fresh air and dive again.

A humpback whale calf stays close to its mother. Huge humpbacks eat tiny animal plankton that they strain from the water through comblike structures in their mouths.

Paddling hard, the young sea turtle dives in search of food.

Hungry, the sea turtle dives in search of food. The light fades as she descends. The water turns from turquoise to dark blue.

Down, down, the sea turtle goes, feasting on plankton. But she can descend only a few hundred feet. Like the whales, she needs to return to the water's surface to breathe air.

Below the sunlit zone, where the turtle swims, lies most of the ocean. It is cold down there and as black as night—all the way to the bottom.

A deep-sea squid
(right), a lantern fish
(below), and a delicate
jellyfish (bottom)
produce their own
light in special organs
in their bodies.

From out of the darkness
come flashes of light. The lights
belong to deep-ocean creatures.
A squid's eight arms glow
against the black water. Rows
of bright spots decorate the
sides of lantern fish. A delicate
jellyfish pulses past, sporting
tentacles that twinkle like stars.

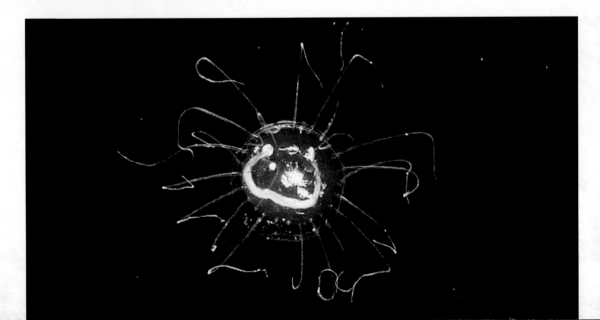

A deep-sea anglerfish hangs motionless in the black water, luring in a meal with light.

The anglerfish uses light to catch its meals. A glowing light sticks out from its forehead, just above its huge mouth. Another light dangles below its body, like a lure on a fishing pole. The lights attract curious fish. When a fish swims in close to investigate the glow, the anglerfish opens wide and swallows.

Tiny copepods swarm like flies in the inky black water of the deep ocean. Plump ctenophores cruise through the swarms, catching dinner as they go.

Snipe eels snake through the dark water. With odd, birdlike beaks, they snag deep-sea shrimp. Even stranger-looking predators, such as gulper eels, lurk in the darkness.

A gulper eel has a huge mouth—big enough to swallow an animal that's bigger than the eel.

Rainbow colors light up the bodies of a tiny copepod (left) and an egg-sized ctenophore (inset).

37

Two thousand . . . five thousand . . . ten thousand feet down—the dark zone of the ocean seems to go on forever. The water is just a few degrees above freezing. Everything is squeezed on all sides by the great weight of billions of gallons of water pressing down. But even on the bottom, miles below the ocean's surface, there is life.

Sea lilies sprout from the ocean floor like strange flowers. A plump sea cucumber plows through the fine sand. These bottom dwellers live on bits of food that drift down from the sunlit zone like falling snow.

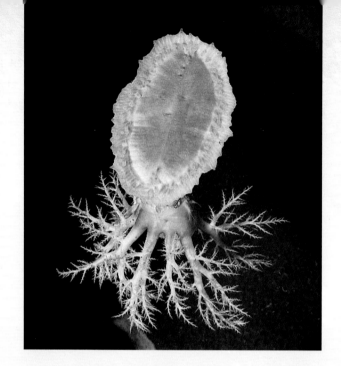

A sea cucumber uses frilly tentacles to search for a meal on the bottom (above). *A sea lily snags food on "arms" that grow in a circle around its mouth* (below).

A brittle star's long arms break off easily, but they quickly grow back again.

A pointy-nosed skate appears, cruising just above the ocean floor. The skate slows and circles over a spot on the bottom. It plunges its head into the sand and comes up with a brittle star in its mouth. But the brittle star breaks free, leaving the skate with a single, wriggling arm for its dinner.

A deep-sea skate glides over the ocean floor, flapping the edges of its body like wings.

The skate moves on. It follows the slant of the ocean floor, going deeper and deeper into frigid darkness. Eleven thousand feet below the ocean's surface, water gushes up from a crack in the ocean floor. The water is very, very hot. It is also rich in chemicals. The crack is called a hydrothermal vent.

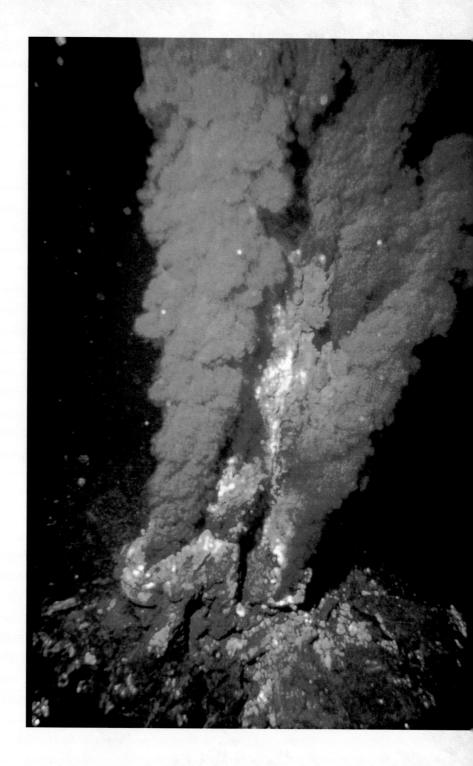

Chemical-rich hot water gushes from a hydrothermal vent like smoke from a chimney.

Microscopic bacteria use the chemicals surging out of the vent to make sugars and other substances that they use for food. Other vent dwellers depend on these bacteria to survive. Some shelter bacteria inside their bodies. Others eat them outright.

Giant clams as big as footballs crowd together near the vent. Parts of the clams' bodies are packed with bacteria. The bacteria make enough food to feed themselves *and* their clam hosts. Small white crabs tiptoe past the clams, nibbling on bacteria that coat the rocks.

Crabs wander among clusters of huge giant clams near a hydrothermal vent.

Giant tube worms
have no mouths.
They get the food
they need from
bacteria that live
inside their bodies.

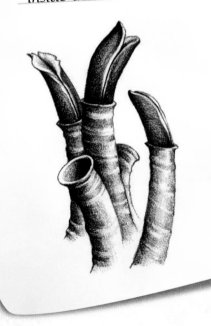

A pale crab climbs through a "forest" of giant tube worms.

Giant tube worms tower above all the other vent creatures. Some tube worms grow taller than a person. Only the lipstick-red tops of their long bodies stick out of the tubes in which they live.

Large crabs live here too. Their spindly legs and bodies are covered with prickly little bumps.

Hydrothermal vent communities are the only communities of living things where bacteria, not plants or algae, form the base of the food web. There is nothing else like them on the earth.

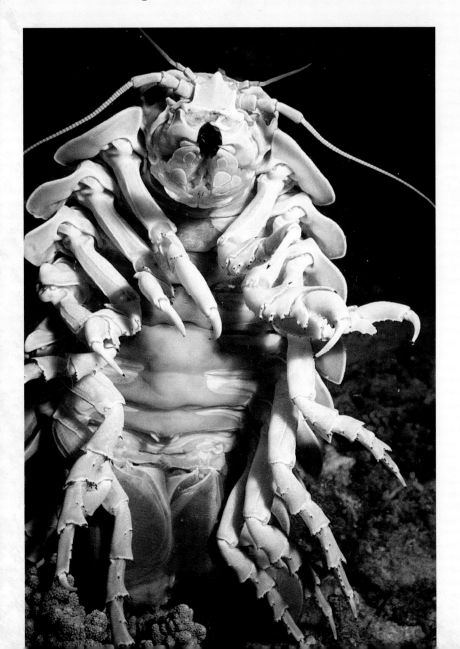

A long-legged crab (above) climbs over rocks—and other vent animals. A visiting giant isopod (left) has even more legs than the crab.

When the sea turtle is about twenty years old, she will return to the beach where she was hatched.

Thousands of feet above the hydrothermal vent, the little sea turtle is swimming through the bright waters near the ocean's surface. She is part of the food web in the ocean's sunlit zone. With luck, she'll avoid being eaten and grow up to be large and strong.

One day, many years from now, she will start on another great ocean journey. This one will take her from the open ocean back toward land. Eventually, she will swim into shallow water close to a shore. It won't be just any shore, though. It will be the very same sandy shore where she hatched from an egg.

One night, the turtle will crawl out of the water and dig a hole in the sand. In it, she'll lay several dozen round, white eggs. After covering the eggs with sand, she will turn and crawl down the beach. Without looking back, she will head into the waves and return to her ocean home.

The sea turtle lays her eggs in the sand (above) *and then returns to the ocean.*

for further
Information
about the Ocean

Books

Arnold, Caroline. *A Walk on the Great Barrier Reef.* Minneapolis: Carolrhoda Books, 1988.

Berman, Ruth. *Sharks.* Minneapolis: Carolrhoda Books, 1995.

Blum, Mark. *Beneath the Sea in 3-D.* New York: Chronicle Books, 1997.

Cerullo, Mary M. *The Truth about Dangerous Sea Creatures.* New York: Chronicle Books, 2003.

Collard III, Sneed B. *The Deep-Sea Floor.* Watertown, MA: Charlesbridge Publishing, 2003.

Holling, Holling Clancy. *Pagoo.* Boston: Houghton Mifflin, 1957.

Lasky, Kathryn. *Interrupted Journey: Saving Endangered Sea Turtles.* Cambridge, MA: Candlewick Press, 2001.

MacQuitty, Miranda. *Ocean.* New York: DK Publishing, 2000.

MacMillan, Dianne. *Humpback Whales.* Minneapolis: Carolrhoda Books, 2004.

Staub, Frank. *Sea Turtles.* Minneapolis: Lerner Publications, 1994.

Taylor, Leighton. *Jellyfish.* Minneapolis: Lerner Publications, 1998.

Walker, Sally M. *Rays.* Minneapolis: Carolrhoda Books, 2003.

Websites

Jean-Michel Cousteau's Ocean Future's Society: Coral Reef Fun
< http://www.oceanfutures.org/Nemo/index2.html >

Part of the Ocean Future's Society website, this provides links to coral reef information and photos.

Nova Online Adventure: Into the Abyss
< http://www.pbs.org/wgbh/nova/abyss/ >

Follow the daring attempt of an ambitious expedition as it goes a mile and a half beneath the sea to explore hydrothermal vents.

Oceanlink
< http://www.oceanlink.island.net/ >

This site explores the importance of the marine environment and its conservation.

Secrets of the Ocean Realm
< http://www.pbs.org/oceanrealm/ >

This PBS site takes you on an interactive tour through the ocean.

Photo Acknowledgments

The photographs in this book are used with the permission of: Seapics.com (© Doug Perrine, pp. 4–5, 38 (bottom), 44; © Marilyn and Maris Kazmers, p. 17 (inset); © Richard Hermann, p. 18; © Saul Gonor, p. 39); Visuals Unlimited (© Rick Poley, pp. 5 (inset), 12, 19; © A.J. Cunningham, p. 6 (bottom); © Adam Jones, pp. 9 (right), 17; © Lindholm M/R, p. 10; © David Wrobel, pp. 15, 20 (middle), 22, 31; © Link, p. 16; © Science VU, p. 20 (bottom), © Richard Hermann, pp. 21, 29; © Dave Fleetham, p. 26 (top); © Gerald & Buff Corsi, p. 26 (bottom); © Mark E. Gibson, p. 28; © Hugh S. Rose, p. 32; © Brandon D. Cole, p. 33; © HBOI, pp. 35 (all), 36, 37; © Ken Lucas, p. 38 (top); © Science VU/F. Gail-WHOI, p. 41; © Whoi D. Foster, p. 42; Science VU/ © NOAA/OAR/NURP, p. 43 (right); © Inga Spence, p. 45 (both)); Tom Stack and Associates (© Brian Parker, pp. 6 (top), 23 (left, middle), 24 (inset), 27; © TSDAO/NASA, p. 8; © Mark Allen Stack, p. 11; © Tom Stack, pp. 23 (top), 26 (middle); © Mike Severns, p. 24; © Dave Fleetham, p. 25 (both), © Mike Parry, p. 30; © OAR/NOAA/TSDAO, p. 40); Photo Researchers (© John Spragens Jr., p. 7; © Michael P. Gadomski, p. 13 (both); © M.H. Sharp, p. 14); © James P. Rowan, p. 9 (top); Photodisc Royalty Free by Getty Images, p. 9 (left); Dr. Neil Sullivan, University of Southern California/NOAA, p. 20 (top); Peter Arnold, Inc. (© Lynda Richardson, p. 34; © Sea Studios Inc., p. 37 (inset); © Lynn Funkhouser, p. 43 (left)).

Cover Photos: Tom Stack and Associates (© Brian Parker (top), © Mike Parry (bottom)).

Index

Numbers in **bold** refer to photos and drawings.